SC

RECIPES

compiled by

Johanna Mathie

Gude health is
better than wealth.
Scottish Proverb

SALMON

Index

Cover pictures *front:* Tarbert Harbour, Loch Fyne by *David Murray* RA
back: In Glen Lussa, Argyllshire by *E.W. Haselhust* RI

Printed and Published by J. Salmon Ltd., Sevenoaks, England

Smoked Salmon and Haddock Pots

Two of Scotland's finest smoked fish poached in cream. Arbroath 'smokies' if they can be obtained, are wonderful in this dish. For an extra treat, sprinkle a little whisky on top just before serving.

8 oz smoked haddock fillet	**Salt and pepper**
6 oz smoked salmon	**Grated nutmeg**
6 fl oz double cream	**3 oz Scottish cheddar cheese, grated**

Set oven to 400°F or Mark 6. Butter 6 ramekin dishes. Remove the skin and bones from the haddock and flake the flesh. Cut the smoked salmon into pieces. Mix together the haddock and salmon and divide between the ramekin dishes. Season the cream with salt and pepper and pour over the fish. Sprinkle with grated nutmeg and top with grated cheese. Place the ramekin dishes on a baking tray and bake for 15 to 20 minutes until lightly browned and bubbling. Serve with crusty bread. Serves 6.

KISIMUL CASTLE, BARRA, OUTER HEBRIDES

Cullen Skink

This hearty fisherman's soup was traditionally always made with Finnan haddock.

1 large Finnan haddock or
2 large smoked haddock fillets
1 onion, chopped
1 pt full cream milk or buttermilk
½ lb cooked mashed potato
1 oz butter
Salt and pepper

Place the haddock in a large pan with sufficient water to cover. Bring to the boil, add the chopped onion and simmer for 10 to 15 minutes until the fish is cooked. Remove the fish, retaining the stock and flake the flesh from the bones and skin. Set aside the flesh and return the bones and skin to the stock. Re-boil the stock for 30 minutes, then remove from the heat and strain into a clean pan. Add the flaked fish and return to the heat. Add the milk, season with salt to taste and bring to the boil for a few minutes. Stir in the mashed potato, butter and pepper to taste and serve immediately. Serves 4.

Finnan Haddie and Poached Eggs

Finnan haddock takes its name from the village of Findon just down the coast from Aberdeen. This combination makes a wonderful breakfast or light supper dish.

4 half fillets Finnan haddock
2 bay leaves
1 slice lemon
4 eggs
Butter
Grated nutmeg
Salt and pepper

Place the fish, bay leaves and lemon in a pan half filled with cold water. Bring to the boil, cover and simmer for 4 minutes. Remove the fish, set aside and keep warm. Discard the bay leaves and lemon and bring the water back to simmering point. One at a time, break the eggs into a cup and gently slip each one into the water. Poach for 3 minutes, removing with a slotted spoon. Meanwhile, place each piece of warm fish on a plate, add a knob of butter, top with an egg, sprinkle with grated nutmeg and season with salt and pepper. Serves 4.

Prawns in Whisky Cream

The combination of whisky and cream makes a wonderfully rich sauce for this delicious starter.

1 oz butter
1 small onion, finely chopped
12 oz shelled prawns
2 tablespoons whisky
5 fl oz double cream
Salt and pepper
2 oz grated cheese
Chopped parsley to garnish

Butter 6 ramekin dishes. Melt the butter in a pan and fry the onion until soft. Add the prawns and heat through, then add the whisky and cook for a further 2 minutes. Stir in the cream then remove the mixture from the heat before it reaches boiling point. Season to taste and pour into the ramekin dishes. Top with grated cheese and brown under a hot grill. Serve immediately, garnished with chopped parsley. Serves 6.

Partan Bree

This traditional crab soup derives its name from the Gaelic 'Partan', meaning crab and 'Brigh' (prounounced Bree), meaning juice or gravy.

1 large boiled crab (approx. 2 to 3 lb)
3 oz long grain rice
1 pt milk
1 pt chicken stock
½ teaspoon anchovy essence
Salt and pepper
5 fl oz single cream

Remove all the meat from the crab and set aside the flesh from the large claws. In a pan, boil the rice in the milk until soft but take care not to over cook. Add the crab meat (except from the claws) and rub the mixture through a sieve into a clean pan. Bring to the boil gradually whilst stirring in the chicken stock. Remove from the heat, add the anchovy essence and the claw meat and season with salt and pepper to taste. Reheat, stirring in the cream, but do not boil. When hot, serve immediately. Serves 4.

THE QUAYSIDE, CRAIL, FIFE

Fish Sausages

This recipe is based on one found in a 1946 Scottish Women's Rural Institute cook book. It makes a change from fishcakes!

6 oz cooked white fish
2 oz peeled prawns
2 oz mushrooms
2 oz breadcrumbs
2 teaspoons dried parsley
Salt and pepper
2 eggs, lightly beaten
3 oz fine oatmeal
A little flour

Skin the fish and remove any bones. Finely chop the prawns. Chop and fry the mushrooms in a little butter. In a bowl, break up and pound the white fish together with the prawns, cooked mushrooms, breadcrumbs, parsley and seasoning, binding with half the beaten egg. With floured hands form the mixture into 'sausages', then dip in the remaining beaten egg and roll in the oatmeal. Fry in hot shallow oil for about 6 to 7 minutes or until golden brown, turning regularly. Drain on kitchen paper. Serves 4.

Smoked Mackerel Pâté

Smoked mackerel and whisky give a distinctive flavour to this delicious pâté.

12 oz smoked mackerel
4 oz butter
4 oz cream cheese
5 fl oz double cream
1 tablespoon lemon juice
2 tablespoons horseradish sauce
2 tablespoons whisky
Salt and pepper

Skin the mackerel and remove all the bones. Place all the ingredients, except the seasoning, into a blender or food processor and mix to a thickish consistency. Season with salt and pepper to taste. Pack the pâté into a buttered dish and chill in the refrigerator. Serve with oatcakes or hot buttered wholemeal toast. Serves 4.

INVERARAY CASTLE, LOCH FYNE, ARGYLLSHIRE

Baked Herrings in Tomato Sauce

Herrings are Scotland's silver darlings. Apparently, plump Loch Fyne herrings were once cheekily referred to as "Glasgow Magistrates".

½ oz butter
1 small onion, finely chopped
2 rashers bacon, finely diced
½ tin chopped tomatoes
Salt and pepper
6 medium herrings
1 teaspoon anchovy essence
2 tablespoons breadcrumbs

Set oven to 375°F or Mark 5. Melt the butter in a pan and gently fry the onion until soft. Add the diced bacon and cook for 2 minutes. Pour in the tomatoes, cover and simmer for 15 minutes and season to taste. Spread the anchovy essence on the herrings and place them in a shallow ovenproof dish. Cover with the tomato sauce and sprinkle over the breadcrumbs. Bake for 15 to 20 minutes until golden brown. Serve hot with mashed potatoes. Serves 4 - 6.

Cheesy Angels

Scottish smoked oysters are well known for their delicate flavour. Heaven in a bite!

2 oz Scottish cheddar cheese   12 smoked oysters   6 rashers streaky bacon

Divide the cheese into 12 small pieces. Trim the rind from the bacon and cut each rasher in half. Place each oyster on a piece of cheese, wrap tightly with bacon and secure with a cocktail stick. Place under a hot grill, turning once, until the bacon is crisp. Serves 4.

Creamy Seafood Curry

Curry has long been a particular Scottish favourite and for a mild curry, seafood is the ideal ingredient.

2 oz butter
2 teaspoons mild curry powder
8 oz haddock fillets, skinned and flaked
4 oz scallops, quartered
4 oz peeled prawns
2 tablespoons flour
2 fl oz white wine
4 fl oz fish or chicken stock
4 fl oz single cream

Melt the butter in a pan, add the curry powder and stir for 2 minutes over a moderate heat to release the flavours. Add the haddock, scallops and prawns and cook for 2 to 3 minutes, then sprinkle over the flour, stir in the wine and cook for a further minute before adding the stock. Continue cooking for a further 2 minutes then stir in the cream and bring the mixture back to heat. Serve hot with boiled rice or creamy mashed potato or, cooled, as a delicious stuffing for pancakes or omelettes. Serves 4.

Baked Salmon with Tarragon

Salmon can dry out very easily when cooking. Sealing it inside a foil parcel keeps it moist.

4 salmon fillets
1 small onion, finely chopped
2 rashers bacon, diced
1/4 teaspoon dried tarragon
2 tablespoons lemon juice
Large sheet of buttered kitchen foil
Double cream or creme fraiche for serving

Set oven to 400°F or Mark 6. Melt the butter in a pan and cook the onion until soft. Add the bacon and tarragon and cook for 2 minutes, then stir in the lemon juice. Lay a sufficiently large piece of foil in an ovenproof dish and arrange on it the salmon fillets, covering them with the onion and bacon mixture. Fold up the sides and seal to make a parcel. Bake for 15 to 20 minutes. Delicious served with a teaspoonful of thick cream or creme fraiche on each fillet. Serves 4.

DRYING NETS AT MALLAIG, INVERNESS-SHIRE

Potted Shrimps

The delicate flavour of shrimps makes this a delightful starter or snack dish.

4 oz butter
1 lb peeled shrimps
Pinch of ground mace
Pinch of ground nutmeg
Salt and pepper
2 - 3 oz melted butter to seal

Melt the butter in a pan over a moderate heat and then add the shrimps, mace, nutmeg and salt and pepper to taste. Heat gradually but do not allow the mixture to boil or the shrimps will be tough. Put the mixture into small ramekin dishes or pots and cover each with enough of the melted butter to exclude the air. Chill in the refrigerator.

'Rumbled' Smoked Salmon

This dish takes its name from 'Rumbledethumps', a Border dish of potatoes and cabbage; the addition of smoked salmon and cream turns it into something special.

3 oz butter
1 small onion, finely chopped
1 lb cooked mashed potato
8 oz cooked cabbage
Salt and pepper
6 oz sliced smoked salmon
3 fl oz soured cream

Set oven to 375ºF or Mark 5. Grease a large baking tray. Melt the butter in a pan and fry the onion until soft and golden, taking care not to let it burn. Remove from the heat, add the cooked cabbage and mashed potatoes, season with the salt and pepper and mash well. Shape into rounds 3/4 inch thick and to a size as may be preferred. Place the rounds on the baking tray and cook for 10 to 15 minutes depending on their size, then allow to cool. To serve, place a folded slice of smoked salmon on each round and top with a teaspoonful of soured cream. Serves 4 - 6.

LERWICK FROM FORT CHARLOTTE, SHETLAND ISLANDS

Fishie Tatties

A simple way to use up left-over fish.

4 large baking potatoes
2 oz butter
1 teaspoon anchovy essence
Left-over cooked fish, as available
2 oz Scottish cheddar cheese, grated

Bake the potatoes in their jackets until crisp on the outside but soft inside. Cut each one in half, scoop out the flesh and put into a bowl with the butter, anchovy essence and cooked fish. Mix thoroughly and replace in the potato jackets. Sprinkle with grated cheese and place under a hot grill until browned on top and heated through. Serves 4.

Creamy Fish Brose

Brose is traditionally a mixture of oatmeal, butter and salt and gives this dish its name. It is a meal in itself.

2 carrots
1 small white turnip
2 sticks celery
1 medium onion
1 leek
2 oz butter
1 oz medium oatmeal
1½ pts fish or chicken stock or water
2 lb white fish fillets
Salt and pepper
5 fl oz single cream

Cut the carrots, turnip and celery into matchsticks. Finely slice the onion and leek. Melt the butter in a large pan, add all the vegetables and sweat, with the lid on, for 5 minutes. Stir in the oatmeal and cook for a further 2 minutes. Add the stock and bring back to the boil, stirring continuously. Reduce the heat and simmer for 10 minutes. Then add the fish, season with salt and pepper and cook gently for a further 15 minutes. Finally stir in the cream and heat through. Serve hot with crusty bread. Serves 4-6.

For a special treat, top with sliced mushrooms previously gently fried in butter.

Tweed Kettle

An all-in-one adaptation of a recipe popular in 19th century Edinburgh, which would have used fresh salmon from the River Tweed. An ideal way to poach salmon.

3 lb fresh salmon (tail end)
1 medium onion, chopped
2 bay leaves
12 peppercorns
Pinch of ground mace
$^1/_2$ pt white wine
Water as required

Place the cleaned salmon in a fish kettle. Add the onion, bay leaves, peppercorns, mace and wine. Pour over enough water to cover the fish and bring to the boil very slowly. Simmer for about 2 to 3 minutes. Remove from the heat and allow the fish to cool in the water, by which time the salmon will be cooked perfectly. Serves 10-12.

Herrings in Oatmeal

This is the definitive Scottish way to cook herrings. Usually, a little lemon juice and parsley are all that is needed to serve as an accompaniment.

4 fresh herrings, gutted
4 oz medium oatmeal
Salt and pepper
2 oz butter

Bone the herrings as follows. Remove the tails and fins with a sharp knife. With a pair of kitchen scissors cut the fish along its underside. Turn it flesh side down and flatten out the fish with a rolling pin, pressing firmly down on the backbone to loosen it from the flesh. Turn the fish over and remove the backbone, easing it away carefully, beginning from the head end. This is made easier if the head has been left on in the gutting. Rinse and dry with kitchen paper. Season the oatmeal with a pinch of salt and pepper and roll the herrings in the oatmeal. Heat the butter in a frying pan and fry the fish, flesh side down first. Cook for 6 to 7 minutes, turning over halfway through cooking. Serve immediately. Serves 4.

HERRING BOATS AT WICK, CAITHNESS

Creamy Lemon Mussels

The lemon and cream complement beautifully the flavour of the mussels in this simple dish.

2 pints mussels
1 oz butter
1 small onion, finely chopped
Juice of 2 lemons
Grated rind of 1 lemon
Knob of butter
½ pint double cream
3 tablespoons chopped parsley

Wash and scrub the mussels under cold running water, discarding any with broken shells or those that do not close when tapped. Remove the beards. Melt the butter in a pan and cook the onion gently until transparent. Add the lemon juice, grated lemon rind and the mussels. Cover the pan and cook quickly, shaking, until the mussels have opened. Strain the mussels, reserving the liquid, place them in a large serving dish and keep warm. Discard any mussels that have not opened. Return the reserved liquid to the pan with a knob of butter, add the cream and cook for 5 minutes until slightly thickened. Pour the sauce over the mussels and sprinkle with chopped parsley. Serve with crusty bread. Serves 4.

Smoked Salmon Tart

Smoked salmon and eggs complement each other beautifully.
Use wild salmon for an even more delicate flavour.

PASTRY

8 oz flour   Pinch of salt   2 oz lard   2 oz butter
2 oz Scottish cheddar cheese, grated   Water to mix

FILLING

3 eggs   5 fl oz double cream   Salt and pepper   8 oz smoked salmon
1 tablespoon chopped chives

Set oven to 350ºF or Mark 4. Grease an 8 inch flan dish. Sift the flour and salt into a bowl, then rub in the lard and butter until the mixture resembles fine bread-crumbs. Add the cheese and enough water to mix to a dough. Cover with clingfilm and chill in the refrigerator for 30 minutes. Roll out the dough on a lightly floured surface, line the flan dish, fill with baking beans and bake blind until light brown. Allow to cool. Break the eggs into a bowl, add the cream and seasoning and whisk together. Spread the salmon over the base of the pastry, sprinkle with chives and pour in the egg mixture. Bake for about 20 minutes until set and lightly golden. Serves 4 - 6.

ST. ANDREWS HARBOUR TOWARDS THE CATHEDRAL, FIFE

Baked Stuffed Mackerel

Easy to catch and easy to cook, mackerel make a simple and healthy dish.

4 medium mackerel
½ lemon
1 oz butter
1 small onion, finely chopped
8 oz fresh breadcrumbs
2 tablespoons chopped parsley or chives
Salt and pepper
1 egg, beaten
2 oz butter, melted
3 tablespoons flour

Set oven to 375°F or Mark 5. Slit the mackerel from head to tail, clean out thoroughly and remove the backbone. The fishmonger will do this, if required. Rub over with lemon and salt. Melt 1 oz of butter in a pan and fry the onion until transparent, then allow to cool. In a bowl, mix together the breadcrumbs, fried onion and parsley or chives, season with salt and pepper and bind with the beaten egg. Use this mixture to stuff the fish. Melt the 2 oz of butter, then roll the mackerel in the flour and, finally, in the melted butter. Place the fish in an ovenproof dish and bake for 25 to 30 minutes, basting with butter halfway through. Serve with a butter glaze and chopped parsley or chives. Serves 4.

Dill and Cucumber Sauce

A perfect sauce to accompany freshly poached salmon or trout.

3 egg yolks
4 oz butter, softened
Juice of half a lemon
1 teaspoon chopped dill
Salt and pepper
1/2 teaspoon chopped parsley
1/4 cucumber, peeled and finely chopped
3 fl oz double cream, whipped

Put the egg yolks into a bowl, add half the butter, the lemon juice and chopped dill and season with salt and pepper. Blend together until the mixture begins to thicken. Heat some water in a small pan and place the bowl on the pan ensuring it does not touch the water. Over a gentle heat, whisk the sauce continuously until it becomes thick and creamy. Remove from the heat, whisk in the remaining butter, then fold in the parsley, chopped cucumber and whipped cream. This makes sufficient sauce for 4 fish.

Fish Cakes

As well as white fish or salmon, smoked fish makes really tasty fish cakes. Also try other herb flavours; salmon marries well with a little tarragon or dill.

8 oz cooked flaked fish, white, smoked or salmon 1 lb potatoes, cooked and mashed
1 oz butter, melted 1 egg, beaten 1 teaspoon chopped parsley Salt and pepper

COATING

1 egg, beaten 4 oz dried breadcrumbs Vegetable oil for frying

In a bowl, mix together the fish, mashed potatoes, melted butter, beaten egg and parsley and season to taste. Place in the refrigerator to chill for about half an hour. Turn out on to a floured surface and roll into a thick sausage shape. Slice and shape into 8 rounds. Dip into the beaten egg, coat with breadcrumbs and shallow fry in hot fat for approximately 5 minutes on each side or until golden brown. Serves 4.

Oaty Crusted Fish Pie

With this alternative recipe for fish pie, the oat crust gives the pie a delicious crunchy texture.

2 oz butter 2 tablespoons flour ½ pint milk 1¼ lb white fish fillets
1 tablespoon chopped parsley 2 hard boiled eggs, chopped
1 tablespoon chopped chives

PASTRY

4 oz flour 2 oz quick porridge oats Salt 3 oz butter or margarine
Beaten egg to glaze Handful of oats for sprinkling

Set oven to 350ºF or Mark 4. Skin the fish, remove any bones and chop into pieces. Melt the butter in a pan, stir in the flour and cook for 1 minute, then gradually add the milk and bring to the boil, whisking constantly until the sauce is thickened. Add the fish, parsley, chives and chopped eggs and then transfer to a buttered baking dish to cool. For the pastry, mix together in a bowl the flour, oats and a pinch of salt, then rub in the butter or margarine. Stir in sufficient cold water to form a stiff consistency. Roll out the pastry on a lightly floured surface to make a lid to cover the baking dish. Trim and crimp the edges and brush with beaten egg. Sprinkle the top with oats and bake for 20 to 25 minutes until light golden brown. Serves 4 - 6.

BRODICK FROM THE PIER, ISLE OF ARRAN

Smoked Trout Pâté

A very quick and tasty pâté for which either sea trout or fresh water trout can be used.

2 fillets smoked trout, skinned   8 oz cream cheese   3 oz butter
Juice of 1 lemon   Dash of tabasco sauce

HORSERADISH MAYONNAISE
3 tablespoons mayonnaise $^{1}/_{4}$ teaspoon horseradish sauce

Place the trout, cream cheese, butter, lemon juice and tabasco sauce in a blender or food processor and blend until smooth. Divide the mixture equally between 4 ramekin dishes and chill in the refrigerator. For the horseradish mayonnaise mix together the 3 tablespoons of good mayonnaise with $^{1}/_{4}$ teaspoon horseradish sauce (the amount of horseradish used can be increased according to taste) and put into a serving pot. To serve, spread the pâté on hot toast and top with a little of the horseradish mayonnaise. Serves 4.

Curried Kedgeree

A delicious and mildly spicy alternative to plain kedgeree.

6 oz long grain rice
12 oz smoked haddock
2 hard boiled eggs
4 oz butter
2 oz raisins
1 level teaspoon curry powder
4 tablespoons single cream
Salt and pepper
Chopped parsley to garnish

Cook the rice in boiling salted water until tender then strain, set aside and keep warm. Poach or grill the haddock until it is just cooked and tender. Remove the skin and bones and flake the flesh. Chop the hard boiled eggs. Melt the butter in a pan and add the fish, chopped eggs and the raisins. Sprinkle in the curry powder, stir and heat through. Add the cream, cook for 2 minutes and season to taste. Arrange the rice in a serving dish, pile on the fish mixture and garnish with chopped parsley. For a very authentic Eastern flavour, add chopped fresh coriander. Serves 4.

HERRING GUTTERS AT WORK, STORNOWAY, ISLE OF LEWIS

Potted or Soused Herrings

An excellent and simple cold dish, which works equally well with mackerel.

8 small fresh herrings, gutted
Salt and pepper
1 large onion, finely sliced
2 bay leaves
10 peppercorns
2 cloves
1/4 pt water
1/4 pt malt vinegar
1/2 teaspoon granulated sugar

Set oven to 325° or Mark 3. Bone the herrings (see Herrings in Oatmeal recipe for method) and sprinkle with salt and ground pepper. Tightly roll up the herrings from head to tail, skin side outwards and arrange in a medium size ovenproof dish. Cover with the sliced onion and add the bay leaves, peppercorns and cloves. Mix together the water, vinegar and sugar and pour over the fish. Cover and bake for 30 to 35 minutes. Allow the herrings to cool in the cooking liquid, then drain and chill before serving. Serves 4.

Partan Pie

This Scottish dish is a simple but delicious way of serving hot dressed crab.

1 cooked crab (approx. 2 to 3 lb)
½ teaspoon grated nutmeg
Salt and pepper
3 tablespoons white wine vinegar
1½ tablespoons mild mustard
2 oz breadcrumbs
1 oz butter for dotting

Remove the crab meat from the shell. In a bowl, mix the crab meat and nutmeg and season with salt and pepper to taste. Mix the vinegar and mustard together in a pan, bring to the boil, stirring gently, then pour over the crab meat mixture. Return the crab meat to the shell and sprinkle over the breadcrumbs. Dot with butter and place under a grill until browned on top and heated through. Serves 2.

Ham and Haddie Layer

Smoked haddock and bacon are natural partners.

½ oz butter
1 small onion, chopped
4 oz bacon, chopped
8 oz tomatoes, sliced
12 oz smoked haddock
2 - 3 tablespoons water
2 oz breadcrumbs
2 oz Scottish cheddar cheese, grated

Set oven to 375°F or Mark 5. Grease a medium size ovenproof dish. Melt the butter in a pan and fry the onion until soft. Add the bacon and cook for a further 2 to 3 minutes. Arrange half of the tomato slices in the dish and cover with the onion and bacon mixture. Place the haddock on top of this layer and top with the remaining tomato slices. Pour on the water and sprinkle with the breadcrumbs and cheese. Cover with a lid or kitchen foil and cook for 20 minutes. Remove the lid or foil and cook for about a further 10 minutes until the topping is browned. Serves 4.

Scallops and Onion Stew

Scallops stewed in their own juice with an onion and cream sauce; a lovely supper dish.

12 scallops 6 tablespoons dry white wine 1/4 pt water Salt and pepper

SAUCE

1 1/2 oz butter 1 small onion, finely chopped 1 tablespoon flour
5 tablespoons single cream 1 1/2 oz breadcrumbs 2 oz Scottish cheddar cheese, grated

Butter an ovenproof dish. Quarter the scallops, place in a pan, cover with the wine and water, season and bring to the boil. Simmer for about 8 minutes, then strain and reserve the liquid. Melt the butter in another pan and gently fry the onion until transparent. Stir in the flour and cook for one minute. Pour in the reserved fish liquid, bring to the boil and simmer for 3 minutes. Add the scallops and cream and reheat, without boiling. Transfer to the ovenproof dish and sprinkle with the breadcrumbs and cheese mixed together. Brown under a hot grill and serve immediately with creamy mashed potato. Serves 4.

THE HARBOUR, HELMSDALE, SUTHERLAND

Easy Fish Pie

Everyone has a favourite recipe for fish pie; this simple recipe is best served with green vegetables.

1 lb haddock	**1 oz flour**
3/4 pt milk	**1 tablespoon chopped parsley**
1 1/2 lbs potatoes, peeled	**Salt and pepper**
1 oz butter	**Butter for dotting**

Set oven to 350°F or Mark 4. Put the fish in an ovenproof dish with the milk, cover and cook for about 20 minutes. Meanwhile, boil the potatoes in salted water until tender, mash with a knob of butter and season with pepper to taste. Drain the cooked fish and reserve the liquid for the sauce. Remove the skin and bones and flake the fish. Melt the butter in a pan, add the flour and cook, stirring, for one minute. Stir in the fish liquid and whisk over a low heat until thickened, then add the fish and chopped parsley and season to taste. Transfer the mixture to a baking dish and cover with a layer of mashed potato. Dot with butter and place under a hot grill until golden brown. Serves 4.

Marinated Kipper Fillets

Kippers are, properly, kippered or smoked herrings. The fish are gutted, split and smoked flat. Scottish kippers are particularly delicious and are best if pale in colour.

4 kipper fillets
1 small onion, thinly sliced
A bay leaf
4 tablespoons vegetable oil
1 level tablespoon caster sugar
3 tablespoons white wine vinegar
Salt and pepper

Peel the skin from the kippers and place the flesh in a shallow dish. Spread with the sliced onion and lay on the bay leaf. For the marinade mix together the oil, sugar and vinegar and season with salt and pepper. Spoon the marinade over the kippers and leave for 10 to 12 hours. Drain and serve with thin slices of brown bread and butter. Serves 4.

THE FISH MARKET, ABERDEEN

Cod in Egg Sauce

Egg sauce is the perfect accompaniment for fresh cod and was also traditionally used in the salted cod dish 'Cabbie Claw'.

4 cod fillets   2 oz butter   2 oz flour   1¼ pts milk
3 hard boiled eggs, finely chopped   1 tablespoon melted butter
Pinch of nutmeg   Salt and pepper

Set oven to 375°F or Mark 5. Butter an overproof dish and arrange in it the cod fillets. Melt the butter in a pan, add the flour and stir in over a low heat. Add the milk gradually, whisking continuously until smooth and creamy. Continue to cook gently for 2 to 3 minutes, then mix in the eggs, the additional tablespoon of melted butter and the nutmeg and season to taste. Stir well over a low heat. Pour the egg sauce over the cod fillets and bake for 20 minutes. Serve with mashed potato. Serves 4.

Mussel Brose

This traditional brose gives a true taste of the sea.

2 pints mussels
$^3/_4$ pt water
8 fl oz milk
1 medium onion, finely chopped
Salt and pepper
2 level tablespoons oatmeal, toasted
4 fl oz single cream, optional if desired

Wash and scrub the mussels under cold, running water, discarding any which do not close when tapped. Remove the beards. Put into a large pan with the water, cover and simmer gently until all the mussels are open. Strain the liquid into a clean pan and shell the mussels. Discard any that have not opened. Add the milk to the mussel liquid with the chopped onion and shelled mussels and season to taste. Heat gently until hot but do not allow the soup to boil. Meanwhile, toast the oatmeal by spreading it out on kitchen foil and brown lightly under a hot grill, but watch closely so it does not burn. Put the toasted oatmeal into a bowl and pour in about $^1/_2$ pint of the mussel liquid, stirring quickly so the oatmeal coagulates into small lumps. Add these 'dumplings' to the soup and serve hot. For a richer soup, the cream may be added just before serving. Serves 3 - 4.

Creamy Finnan Haddie

Finnan Haddies have a lovely, subtle flavour which is ideal for this dish. However, other smoked haddock can be substituted if necessary.

2 Finnan haddock or 4 medium smoked haddock fillets
1 pt milk   A bay leaf   6 peppercorns   2 oz butter   2 tablespoons flour
2 heaped teaspoons mustard powder   5 fl oz double cream

Divide the fish into 4 pieces if necessary and put into a large pan. Cover with the milk, add the bay leaf and peppercorns and bring to the boil. Reduce the heat and simmer gently until the fish is cooked. Carefully lift out the fish with a slotted spoon, drain and place in a heated, shallow serving dish. Cover and keep warm. Strain the fish milk into a container. Melt the butter in a pan, stir in the flour and mustard powder and cook for 2 minutes. Add the fish milk and bring to the boil, stirring continuously, until it thickens. Remove from the heat and stir in the cream. Reheat, but do not allow to boil, and pour over the fish. Serve with boiled potatoes and a green vegetable. Serves 4.

METRIC CONVERSIONS

The weights, measures and oven temperatures used in the preceding recipes can be easily converted to their metric equivalents. The conversions listed below are only approximate, having been rounded up or down as may be appropriate.

Weights

Avoirdupois	Metric
1 oz.	just under 30 grams
4 oz. (¼ lb.)	app. 115 grams
8 oz. (½ lb.)	app. 230 grams
1 lb.	454 grams

Liquid Measures

Imperial	Metric
1 tablespoon (liquid only)	20 millilitres
1 fl. oz.	app. 30 millilitres
1 gill (¼ pt.)	app. 145 millilitres
½ pt.	app. 285 millilitres
1 pt.	app. 570 millilitres
1 qt.	app. 1.140 litres

Oven Temperatures

	°Fahrenheit	Gas Mark	°Celsius
Slow	300	2	150
	325	3	170
Moderate	350	4	180
	375	5	190
	400	6	200
Hot	425	7	220
	450	8	230
	475	9	240

Flour as specified in these recipes refers to plain flour unless otherwise described.